The

369

JOURNAL

ALSO BY KEILA SHAHEEN

The Shadow Work Journal

The Vibrational Poetry Book

The Lucky Girl Journal

The

369

JOURNAL

Neuroscience-Based Journaling:
Your Key to Unlocking Limitless Potential with Numerology

Keila Shaheen

ONE PLACE. MANY STORIES

HQ
An imprint of HarperCollins*Publishers* Ltd
1 London Bridge Street
London SE1 9GF

www.harpercollins.co.uk

HarperCollins*Publishers*
Macken House, 39/40 Mayor Street Upper,
Dublin 1, Ireland, D01 C9W8

This edition 2024

1
First published in Great Britain by
HQ, an imprint of HarperCollins*Publishers* Ltd 2024

ISBN 978-0-00-873006-2

This book contains FSC™ certified paper and other controlled
sources to ensure responsible forest management.

For more information visit: www.harpercollins.co.uk/green

Printed and bound in the UK using 100% Renewable
Electricity at CPI Group (UK) Ltd

The
369
JOURNAL

Belongs to _____

DOWNLOAD
the APP

SCAN HERE

WHERE TECHNOLOGY
MEETS INNER TRANSFORMATION.

- Track triggers

- Check in feelings

- Journal prompts

- Healing exercises

- View emotional patterns over time

IF ONLY YOU KNEW THE MAGNIFICENCE OF THE NUMBERS 3, 6, AND 9, THEN YOU WOULD HAVE THE KEY TO THE UNIVERSE.

—NIKOLA TESLA

DECLARATION *of* INTENT

I, _____, vow on this day to commit
to my personal growth. I promise to fill in every blank page until
they are completed, and I promise to love and embrace myself fully
throughout the process. I understand that life is ever-changing, and
I will not forget that I hold the wisdom and strength to overcome all
obstacles. I am grateful for this magical moment and look forward
to the revelations I'll discover in the days ahead.

_____

SIGNATURE

_____

START DATE

_____

COMPLETION DATE

This is your 369 Journal.

You will use it to keep track of your goals,
take inspired action daily, and align
with the frequencies of the universe.

Pay attention to your energy and watch it transmit
abundance, success, and creativity in your life.

Ready? Let us begin.

CONTENTS

1

Introduction

The 369 Journal

This journal opens a door to a special room in your subconscious that you can visit to align your aspirations and intentions with reality. You will gain clarity around your purpose and goals and lay out the steps needed to achieve them.

On the pages of this journal, you will bring kinetic energy to your thoughts and focused attention, creating the life you wish to experience for yourself. With this 369 Journal, you will experience firsthand the power of manifestation and use it to create a life that is filled with joy, abundance, opportunities, and success.

Remember that the path toward your goals is not always linear and that there will be times when you may feel overwhelmed, stressed, or confused. But with a bit of patience and determination, you can use these pages to turn your setbacks into meaningful lessons and follow your dreams with concrete intentions. Take your time and enjoy the process. Every thought and step you take is an important part of your journey.

What Is the 369 Method?

The 369 Method combines significant numerical patterns with the power of your mind to manifest your dreams into reality. There is a creative reasoning behind this repetitive practice. Patterns are all around us, from the architecture in beautiful buildings to the wellspring of honeycombs in a honeybee hive. Even our very own DNA structure, a spiral pattern, shows you the synchronicity with the patterns of the natural world. In graphic design, designers use the golden ratio—a proportion of 1:1.618—to create brilliant designs by imbuing them with a natural sense of beauty and balance. By aligning the components of an element, such as a logo, according to the golden ratio, designers ensure that each part harmonizes with the whole, leading to a final design that is not only memorable but also visually resonant with their audience.

These patterns around our environment start small and expand into fractals, creating a larger design that our visual eye can digest. The absence of these subtle patterns in our environment significantly unsettles us, even when we're not overtly aware of their impact. These patterns that make up our reality are more than visual aesthetics for us; they hold a key to knowledge and insight into our human psyche. Even more, they serve as a mirror of the interconnectedness of all things that sustain life. So if we apply the art of numerical structure to enhance our external world, what if we applied it to our human design to enhance our internal world? This is one aspiration of the 369 Method.

Given our human tendency to form thought patterns called *habits*, we navigate life through a series of samskaras—deep-seated impressions influenced by our past actions, thoughts, and life experiences. These samskaras shape our beliefs and thoughts and create habits, sometimes misaligning us from our optimal selves. The 369 Method introduces a transformative practice of intentional repetition and systematic writing to program new, constructive intentions into our psyche. This nurtures a mindset more conducive to recognizing opportunities and taking intentional actions, expanding our mental horizons beyond the constraints of previous samskaras.

Frequency matters in manifestation practices, and tapping into these numbers gives you the frequency to uplift your spirits and realign your energy. Frequency is relevant to many subject matters—scientific, technological, spiritual, and philosophical—due to its fundamental nature in describing the oscillations of waves, which are the basis of energy and information transfer in the universe. In science and technology, frequency determines the properties of sound, light, and electromagnetic waves, which allow scientists to analyze how they interact with matter and carry information. For example, light waves determine color, and sound waves affect the pitch we hear.

Your frequency is the vibrational essence of your being. It is the harmony in which your mind and spirit resonate. It is the energy that your presence holds in a room. Think of someone you know whose positive energy transforms a room into a comforting space for laughter and connection. On the other hand, you might know someone with lower frequencies and recall how they drain a room, casting shadows of discomfort and negativity. Scan the QR codes on page 6 to listen to 111 Hz and 114 Hz binaural frequencies, designed to promote deep relaxation and to reduce stress, and the 369 Hz frequency for healing, balancing, and manifesting your intentions.

In neuroscientific discussions of the cognitive functions of the human mind, frequencies are analyzed in the form of brain waves. Brain waves are correlated with different mental states, such as wakeful relaxation (alpha waves), deep sleep (delta waves), and normal conscious waking experience (beta waves). You can change the state you are in by altering your brain-wave patterns. Our frequencies are reflections of our inner states of consciousness, and through practices like meditation, chanting, and the use of singing bowls, for example, we can recalibrate our energies.

When you engross yourself in 369 journaling, you enter a zone of concentration and openness, which means your mind bathes in the tranquility of alpha brain waves, fostering a serene yet alert state. This optimal blend of peace and focus not only sparks creativity but also smooths the way into a flow state, making the act of intentional writing feel seamless and ideas pour out.

By using this simple but powerful method, you will plant seeds of thought and belief into your subconscious mind. Once you complete this journal, you will look back with immense gratitude and awe as you realize how capable you are of shifting your reality. This is one of the most powerful manifestation techniques, but it cannot be done without inspired action. With consistent belief and action, you will accomplish what you once thought was impossible. With the 369 Method, you will manifest anything—wealth, positive relationships, friendships, good health, and so on.

How to Ramp Up Your Personal Vibration

Binaural Beats: This is a practice of utilizing headphones to listen to two tones with slightly different frequencies simultaneously, one in each ear. Binaural beats synchronize brain activity to achieve specific mental states, from deep relaxation to heightened alertness. Visit Zenfulnote's Spotify and YouTube to listen to binaural beat tracks, or simply scan the QR codes on the next page.

Meditation: This is a practice of mindfulness and focused thought that quiets the mind and promotes deep relaxation and awareness. Meditation can significantly improve your mental, emotional, and physical health by aligning your mind, body, and spirit. Visit Zenfulnote's YouTube or download the Zenfulnote app for a library of powerful meditations to try.

Vocals: Singing or chanting acts as a powerful tool for emotional release and expression. It harmonizes body and mind, uplifts your mood, helps you release stuck energy, and allows you to connect with yourself and those around you. Try singing, humming, or sighing to experience this release.

Outdoor Walks: Spending time in nature and engaging with its energy can ground you, providing clarity and a natural uplift in your energy. Walk barefoot, touch a tree, pause, and notice the many plants, insects, and ecosystems thriving around you.

Solfeggio Frequencies: This ancient sonic therapy has tones that are known for their healing and transformative properties, which can support your emotional and spiritual growth.

Color Therapy: Surrounding yourself with colors that resonate with your desired frequencies can influence your mood and energy. Warm colors like red, orange, and yellow tones are positive, energizing, and passionate, while cool colors like green, purple, and blue are typically calming and relaxing.

Dance or Movement: Moving your body with dance or any other form of physical expression can release stagnant energy and align your body's vibrations with your emotional and spiritual needs. Dance, exercise, shaking somatically, and stretching are all potent methods of movement to release and express the current state of emotions you're experiencing.

111 Hz AND 114 Hz
BINAURAL BEATS FOR
DEEP RELAXATION

369 Hz FREQUENCY
FOR HEALING ENERGY
AND MANIFESTATION

SCAN HERE

SCAN HERE

The Father of 369: Nikola Tesla

Nikola Tesla was known for his contributions to inventions that we rely on every day, things like X-rays and the wireless transmission of power, which seemed unimaginable during his time. How could he visualize such a different world at a point in time when people traveled by horse and buggy? For Tesla, the answer lay in the way he imagined the future by tapping into his hidden potential.

He believed that if you integrate 369 into your daily routine, you can unlock your true potential.

Tesla was a Serbian American inventor, electrical engineer, mechanical engineer, and futurist who is best known for his contributions to the design of the modern alternating current (AC) electricity supply system. He was born in 1856 and died in 1943.

Tesla's inventions and discoveries in the fields of electricity and magnetism were numerous and varied. Some of his most notable contributions include the development of the alternating current (AC) motor, which made the widespread distribution of electric power possible, and the design of the Tesla coil, which is still used in radio technology today.

Tesla is widely considered one of the greatest scientists in history. Michael Faraday, another giant in the field, made a groundbreaking discovery in 1831 by demonstrating that electricity could be produced through magnetism with motion, a principle known as electromagnetic induction. Faraday's discovery laid the foundation for the generation of electricity, and it was Tesla who put these principles into large-scale practical use, ultimately transforming how the world generates and uses electrical power.

Tesla's achievement earned him a distinction shared by only two Americans, as a unit of electrical measurement was named after him. Such recognition is given only to a select few scientists. Among the small number of scientists worldwide who have received this honor, Tesla stands out with his fifteen honorary degrees from prestigious universities and fourteen awards of merit from prominent organizations.

He has been called one of the "saints of science," drawing comparison to the illustrious Leonardo da Vinci for his unparalleled contributions and visionary work. Despite his major accomplishments, Tesla is often referred to as the world's greatest forgotten inventor and has been overlooked by the Smithsonian, which gives credit to Thomas Edison for the widespread use of electricity and to Guglielmo Marconi for the invention of radio.

One of Tesla's most notable ideas was his desire for free energy, which he believed could be harnessed from the environment using wireless technology. He spent much of his later years trying to develop a system for the wireless transmission of electricity but was never able to fully realize this goal.

Tesla's ultimate purpose in life was to use the mind to master the material world and harness the forces of nature to human needs.

Tesla believed that the numbers 3, 6, and 9 were related to the principles of vibration and resonance, and that they held the key to understanding the secrets of the universe. He incorporated these numbers into his work, believing that they could even unlock the secrets of how to create and distribute free energy. He would spend hours pacing around a room, visualizing these numbers and their relationships as a way of stimulating his creative thinking.

Mathematical Systems That Govern Nature

Mathematics provides a closer understanding of nature's mysteries. From minute atomic structures to the boundless universe, mathematical principles and constructs define the essence and order of our reality. This section will delve into the fascinating world of the repetitive sequences that govern nature, including sacred geometry and the 369 Method. There are hidden geometrical patterns in the natural world around us. For example, we can see these patterns present in nature in the form of the golden ratio and the Fibonacci sequence.

These mathematical patterns are not just abstract concepts but also are visibly manifested in the growth and structure of living organisms. For instance, the spirals of shells and the arrangement of leaves around a stem follow the Fibonacci sequence, creating a natural efficiency in growth and reproduction. The golden ratio can be observed in the proportions of the human body and in the branching patterns of trees. Multicellular organisms begin their development through the division of a single cell. This single cell divides into two cells, and as the division continues, a complex multicellular organism is formed, showcasing the inherent order within biological processes. By understanding these mathematical patterns, we gain deeper insights into the fundamental workings of life and the world we live in.

The Golden Ratio

The golden ratio, represented by the Greek letter phi (φ), is a fundamental proportion that manifests itself in various natural phenomena, from the spiral arms of galaxies to the branching patterns of trees. This mathematical concept, which can be derived by dividing a line into two distinct segments in such a way that the ratio of the whole line to the larger segment equals the ratio of the larger segment to the smaller segment, has been demonstrated in numerous artistic and architectural masterpieces throughout history, such as the Parthenon in Athens and the painting the *Mona Lisa* by Leonardo da Vinci.

The presence of the golden ratio in both natural and human-made systems has intrigued researchers and artists for centuries. The ratio's aesthetic appeal and harmonious properties have made it a valuable tool in design and composition, and its occurrence in the universe has fueled speculation about its potential role in the creation of the cosmos. The golden ratio is not limited to two-dimensional forms; it is also found in three-dimensional shapes, like the polyhedra known as the icosahedron and the dodecahedron. These geometric forms are closely linked to the structure of viruses and certain carbon-based molecules, which suggests that the golden ratio may play a role in the molecular architecture of life.

The Fibonacci Sequence

The Fibonacci sequence is a mathematical pattern commonly found in nature, appearing everywhere from the growth patterns of plants to the spiral patterns of seashells. It is generated by adding the two preceding numbers, starting with 0 and 1, to form a sequence of numbers: 0, 1, 1, 2, 3, 5, 8, 13, 21, and so on.

The recurrence of the Fibonacci sequence in nature has fascinated scientists and mathematicians. The number of petals on flowers, the branching patterns of trees, and the distribution of seeds in a sunflower all conform to the Fibonacci sequence.

The spirals found in the shells of such sea creatures as the nautilus follow a logarithmic spiral closely related to the Fibonacci sequence. More recently, the Fibonacci sequence has inspired developments in fields such as engineering and computer science. For example, the sequence has been used in the development of algorithms and coding techniques. The connection between this sequence and the golden ratio hints at a deeper relationship between mathematics and the universe.

> *The day science begins to study non-physical phenomena, it will make more progress in one decade than in all the previous centuries of its existence.*
> —NIKOLA TESLA

Vortex Mathematics

Vortex mathematics, also known as vortex-based math, is a system designed to uncover the numerical patterns and relationships that govern the universe. This approach starts with the idea that numbers are not just abstract symbols but dynamic forces that shape our reality. In vortex mathematics, numbers are arranged in a spiral pattern, highlighting the intricate connections between them. A fascinating aspect of vortex math is its repeating pattern: 1, 2, 4, 8, 7, 5. This sequence continues indefinitely, cycling through the same numbers.

If you take a closer look, the numbers 3, 6, and 9 are missing from this pattern. Scientist Marko Rodin has suggested that these numbers represent a vector from the third to the fourth dimension, which he calls a "flux field." According to Rodin, this field is a higher-dimensional energy that influences the energy circuit of the other six points. He believes that understanding this flux field could be the key to unlocking free energy—a concept that Nikola Tesla devoted a great part of his life to mastering.

By exploring vortex mathematics, we can begin to decode the hidden numerical patterns that underpin the universe. This understanding might lead to revolutionary advancements in energy and other fields and an expansion of the pioneering work of Tesla.

Tesla's theory was that 1, 2, 4, 8, 7, and 5 represent the physical world in which we live. Conversely, the numbers 3, 6, and 9 represent a vector into the fourth dimension. He speculated that by understanding and harnessing these numerical keys, you could tap into this vast unseen reservoir of power and information, unlocking new technologies and generating profound advancements in science. Tesla's methods for accessing and implementing knowledge gained from this higher-dimensional space involved deep intuition, complex mathematical calculations, and innovative experiments aimed at creating inventions that could harmonize with the fundamental frequencies of the universe. Sacred geometry serves as a bridge between the physical and metaphysical realms, guiding us toward an understanding of the divine order.

> We are whirling through the endless space with inconceivable speed. All around us everything is spinning, everything is moving, everywhere there is energy. There must be some way of availing ourselves of this energy more directly. Then, with the light obtained from the medium, with the power derived from it, with every form of energy obtained without effort, from the store forever inexhaustible, humanity will advance with giant strides. The mere contemplation of these magnificent possibilities expands our minds, strengthens our hopes, and fills our hearts with supreme delight.
> —NIKOLA TESLA, 1891

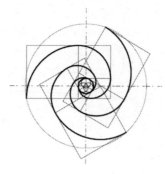

Why 369?

The numbers 3, 6, and 9 show up in the universe and in nature consistently in a very significant way.

If we take a perfect circle's digital root, we are left with:

3 + 6 + 0 = 9
A circle has 360 degrees.

If you split a circle in half, you get 180 degrees.

The digital root of 180 = 9.
180/2 = 90
The digital root of 90 is 9.
If you split 90 in half, you get 45.

The digital root of 45 is 9.
If you split 45 in half, you get 22.5.
2 + 2 + 5 = 9
If you split 22.5 in half, you get 11.25.

1 + 1 + 2 + 5 = 9
No matter how you continue to split the degrees, the digital root always results in 9.

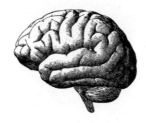

The Science of Habit

The process of building habits is an important aspect of human behavior. It has been studied by psychologists, sociologists, and economists, as well as other behavioral scientists. Habits are a part of our everyday lives and have a powerful influence on our behavior and our experiences. A habit is a behavior repeated so often that it becomes automatic and is difficult to change. Habits can be both helpful and harmful and can be either conscious or subconscious.

Habits are formed through the process of classical conditioning, which is when a behavior is associated with a particular stimulus. This is usually done through repetition and reinforcement. The prefrontal cortex is responsible for the conscious effort to create new habits or change existing ones. Building new habits requires both the repetition of the behavior and the conscious effort to initiate the behavior.

The 369 Method is incredibly powerful because it helps you decondition harmful subconscious habits and replace them with new, positive ones through repetitive scripting and consistent goal-oriented actions. By using this journal daily, you will cognitively restructure your beliefs about your own potential. In turn, this will affect how you perform throughout the day positively.

Pathways

Neuropathways connect relatively distant areas of the brain or nervous system. Each pathway is associated with a particular action or behavior.

Every time we think, do, or feel something, we strengthen this pathway. *Habits* are well-traveled pathways. Our brain finds these things easy to do.

Neuroplasticity

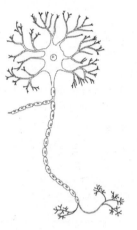

New thoughts and skills carve out new pathways.

Repetition and practice strengthen these pathways, forming new habits.

Old pathways get used less and weaken.

Strengthening of Neural Connections

Neurons wire together to make more lasting circuits.

Mental Activity

This can be a thought, a feeling, and/or an action.

Repetition of Mental Activity

Consistent repetition of a thought, a feeling, and/or an action.

Creation of New Neural Structures

Neurons fire together, forming a brief connection by communication through gaps called synapses.

With attention and repetition, you can change your brain and nervous system by thinking and feeling how you want your life to be.

The Power of Writing

Writing something down repeatedly is a proven technique to help your brain grow and manifest things in your life. It's a form of cognitive training that helps you focus your attention and create better neural pathways in your brain. When you write something down repeatedly, you are engaging in a form of repetitive learning, which helps you remember and understand the information.

Writing on paper also helps you to create a plan and take steps to achieve a goal. By focusing your attention on the goal, you create a vision for yourself that can be seen and understood, making it easier to stay motivated and on track.

By regularly noting down your ambitions, you ease the path to their realization. This cognitive practice propels you toward achieving what you desire and also amplifies your capacity to bring these outcomes into existence.

When goals seem too lofty or distant, writing them down transforms abstract aspirations into concrete plans, engaging the brain's powerful mechanisms of visualization and intention setting. This act stimulates the prefrontal cortex, the brain's planning and decision-making hub, enhancing focus and clarity. Neurologically, it also activates the reticular activating system (RAS), which helps filter information relevant to your goals, making you more attuned to opportunities and actions in alignment with your objectives. Through this process, the brain starts to see the means to achieve these goals as attainable, adjusting your cognitive framework and motivation accordingly.

How to Use This Book

How do I do the 369 Method?
Write your goal down three times in the morning, six times in the afternoon, and nine times in the evening. Then take inspired action during the day.

Do I start with affirming my goals or listing my actions?
Start by putting your goals down in an affirmations format. This will help prime your subconscious and build emotions associated with your desire.

Do I have to write the same thing down for the entire book?
No, you do not. You can change the way you phrase your goal, and you can change your goal entirely. Throughout your journey, new ideas will come, and you may gain more clarity about what you want in life.

Can I manifest multiple things at once?
Yes, you can. If you would like to manifest two things, use two separate pages so you can keep your intentions organized.

Do I have to write my desire down at certain times of the day?
No, you do not. We recommend that you write in the morning, afternoon, and evening. However, it is acceptable and still effective if you choose to write down all your goals at once in the morning.

What can I pair with this book to help me achieve my goals?
Listen to sound healing frequencies and Solfeggio frequencies on your headphones, repeat positive affirmations, meditate, exercise, and incorporate movement throughout your day. Listening to an inspiring song while you are writing your desires will amplify your practice even more.

What if I miss a day?
It is okay if you miss a day. You can always pick the practice back up again!

The 369 Method

Write your desire three times in the morning.

✦ ✦ ✦

Write your desire six times in the afternoon.

✦ ✦ ✦ ✦ ✦ ✦

Write your desire nine times in the evening.

✦ ✦ ✦ ✦ ✦ ✦ ✦ ✦ ✦

"I am so happy and my heart is so full now that I have
$10,000 extra in my checking account."

Example of 369 Method

MORNING ☀️

I got a promotion this week.

I got a promotion this week.

I got a promotion this week.

AFTERNOON ☀️

I got a promotion this week.

I got a promotion this week.

I got a promotion this week.

I got a promotion this week.

I got a promotion this week.

I got a promotion this week.

EVENING 🌙✨

I got a promotion this week.

I got a promotion this week.

I got a promotion this week.

I got a promotion this week.

I got a promotion this week.

I got a promotion this week.

I got a promotion this week.

I got a promotion this week.

I got a promotion this week.

369 Method, Example 2

MORNING ☼

I attract loving and supportive relationships into my life.
I attract loving and supportive relationships into my life.
I attract loving and supportive relationships into my life.

AFTERNOON ☀

I attract loving and supportive relationships into my life.
I attract loving and supportive relationships into my life.
I attract loving and supportive relationships into my life.
I attract loving and supportive relationships into my life.
I attract loving and supportive relationships into my life.
I attract loving and supportive relationships into my life.

EVENING ☾✧✧

I attract loving and supportive relationships into my life.
I attract loving and supportive relationships into my life.
I attract loving and supportive relationships into my life.
I attract loving and supportive relationships into my life.
I attract loving and supportive relationships into my life.
I attract loving and supportive relationships into my life.
I attract loving and supportive relationships into my life.
I attract loving and supportive relationships into my life.
I attract loving and supportive relationships into my life.

Tips to Amplify Your 369 Practice

- Pick one thing you would like to manifest into your life. Write what you want as if it has already happened three, six, and nine times throughout your day. Make sure to be very specific with your goals.

- Phrase your goals as affirmations, as though you have the thing you're manifesting and are grateful for it. For example: "I am so grateful and my heart is so full that I received $1,000 this week."

- Use phrases like I am, I have, and I will in your affirmations. Avoid phrases like I need and I want; such statements create a sense of longing and lack. You want to come from a place of abundance and fulfillment.

- Use the Abraham-Hicks's 17-Second Rule: After each day of 369 affirmations, take seventeen seconds to visualize your desire. How does it feel? Who would you tell the good news about achieving your goal to? Can you picture in detail where you would be when you share the information? What would the setting look like? What would you say? Surrender to the creative power of your imagination.

- Focus on the emotions that your desired reality will evoke. Visualize your goals coming to fruition and hold on to the feeling this gives you.

- Listen to music during your 369 scripting. Music is a powerful tool for tapping into your emotions during your practice.

- Consider adding grammatic elements, symbols, and doodles to emphasize your feelings of excitement. For example, adding an exclamation mark at the end of your sentence. Or adding doodles like dollar signs, hearts, and any symbols that reflect your desires and feelings around your desires.

How to Pivot

When it comes to affirmations, especially time-specific ones like expecting a raise within a week, flexibility and alignment with broader goals can be more beneficial than sticking rigidly to a specific outcome that doesn't materialize as expected.

If your specific affirmation ("I will get a raise next week") doesn't come to fruition, it could be more effective to pivot or reframe your affirmation rather than repeating the same one. This doesn't mean giving up on your goal but rather approaching it from a mindset open to various outcomes, focusing on the positives already present in your life. Reframing your affirmation to reflect your appreciation of the value of your job can help you stay upbeat and keep you energetically aligned with your broader goals.

Here's a way to reframe your affirmation that keeps it open-ended and focused on the feelings and qualities important to you:

Original Affirmation: "I will get a raise next week."

Reframed Affirmation: "I am deeply appreciated and valued in my job. Every day, I open myself to abundance and new opportunities to grow and prosper."

This reframed affirmation shifts the focus from a specific outcome (getting a raise by a certain time) to an appreciation of your current worth and an openness to various forms of abundance. It's less about forcing a specific event to happen and more about aligning yourself with the emotions and qualities you associate with that event, such as feeling valued, recognized, and financially secure.

By focusing on being valued and appreciated in your job, you're also creating a positive feedback loop that can improve your performance and relationships at work, potentially leading to the outcome you desire in a natural and less pressured way. Remember that affirmations are most powerful when they resonate with you and reflect what you truly desire, not just the surface-level outcome.

Here are other examples of reframing or pivoting your affirmation goals:

Original Goal Affirmation: "I will find my dream job by next month."

Reframed Affirmation: "I am open to discovering new opportunities that align with my passions and skills. Every day I am closer to my ideal career."

Original Goal Affirmation: "I must be in a relationship by the end of the year."

Reframed Affirmation: "I am surrounded by love in various forms. I welcome meaningful connections that foster mutual growth."

Original Goal Affirmation: "I need to save $3,000 by October."

Reframed Affirmation: "I am growing a mindset of abundance and financial wisdom. My decisions support my journey toward financial freedom and security."

If you need an extra boost in times of confusion or struggle during your journey, below is a guided meditation to overcome challenges to support you. Simply scan the QR code to listen.

MEDITATION FOR OVERCOMING
CHALLENGES

SCAN HERE

Harnessing the Light Within You

As we move swiftly through this life, seeking purpose and fulfillment, we often find ourselves yearning for more—more love, success, happiness, and abundance. This innate desire for growth is natural. It's human. It's part of our process of growth and development, not just for our minds but for our souls. This inner growth and fulfillment happens when you set real, concrete intentions in your heart.

Intention is the seed from which the garden of your dreams grows. It is the focused energy that ignites the seed of your desires, adding power and energy to what you truly want most in the core of your being. To manifest effectively, you must cultivate a clear and unwavering intention, a deeper purpose at the root of what you truly want. Begin by identifying your most profound hopes and desires—those that resonate with your soul and align with your life's meaning and impact. Visualize them in vivid detail, allowing your imagination to paint the life you aspire to create.

Don't forget to balance action and surrender. While inspired action is necessary to bring your dreams to fruition, you must also release control and surrender to the flow of life. Allow your intuition to guide your steps, recognizing when to forge ahead and when to pause and reflect. Embrace that things will happen at the right time, and if they don't, you are simply being redirected. Let go and envision your dreams unfolding with a nightly visualization meditation to infuse your subconscious with empowering beliefs and affirmations. Simply scan the QR code below to listen.

SLEEP VISUALIZATION MEDITATION
TO MANIFEST YOUR DREAMS

SCAN HERE

Twenty-Five Ideas for Manifesting

ROMANCE

A deeply nurturing relationship blossoming from mutual respect and understanding.

A marriage that stands the test of time, enriched with shared personal growth.

The joy of conceiving and nurturing a new life with love.

An intimate connection that strengthens your emotional and physical bond.

SPIRITUALITY

Harmonious alignment with your true essence, fostering an authentic life path.

A life threaded with moments of joy, meaningful coincidences, and divine connections.

A sign, symbol, or omen guiding you toward your destiny.

A meaningful encounter with a stranger or old friend.

HEALTH

A balanced weight through wellness and self-care.

Radiant, healthy skin that reflects your inner well-being.

Restorative and deeply restful sleep that rejuvenates your mind and body.

A state of health, vitality, and zest for life.

FINANCIAL

Creating streams of passive income that offer you freedom and security.

Achieving financial autonomy, where your life choices are not constrained by economic factors.

Discovering innovative methods for wealth that align with your passions.

Unexpected financial blessings that bring you joy and ease.

CAREER

Landing a dream job that aligns with your passions and skills.

Ascending to roles of greater responsibility and reward.

Receiving positive recognition for your work contributions.

Courageously embracing a new career path that resonates with your soul's calling.

Successfully launching your entrepreneurial vision.

RELATIONSHIPS

Forming new connections that resonate on a deep, soulful level.

Discovering a kindred spirit who becomes a lifelong friend.

Improving family relationships with patience and unconditional love.

Encountering acts of kindness and generosity that restore your faith in humanity.

2
Affirmations

Affirmations

Welcome to the affirmations section of your 369 Journal. Here, you'll find affirmations designed to help you tap into the powerful energy accessible to you. Take a moment to center yourself. Breathe deeply and clear your mind. As you read each affirmation, say it with conviction and feel its energy resonate within you. If any affirmations feel challenging, repeat them with love and patience. Let these words become a part of your daily life, guiding you to manifest the reality you desire. Embrace this practice and watch as your intentions transform into your everyday experiences.

AFFIRMATION TO MANIFEST WEALTH, HEALTH,
LOVE, AND SUCCESS

SCAN TO LISTEN

Affirmations for Abundance

I don't chase, I attract. What belongs to me will simply find me.

I can do anything I set my mind to.

The world is rigged in my favor.

I accept myself for who I am.

I have the power to create change.

I am grateful for all that I have.

I achieve my goals by taking action.

There is abundance all around me.

Today is the best day of my life.

I attract abundance with my thoughts, words, and actions.

Abundance is my natural state of being.

I am grateful for the abundance that I have.

I am open to new opportunities for abundance.

I attract abundance into my life with joy and love.

I am thankful for the abundance in my life.

I am open to receiving the abundance that the universe has to offer.

I focus on the positive.

I deeply love and accept myself.

Affirmations for Relationships

I am ready for a loving relationship.

I am grateful for my past relationships.

I've done the work to accept myself, and now I'm ready for love.

I release all separation and judgment.

I'm willing to view others with love and kindness.

Relationships are mirrors of my ability to love myself.

Loving myself allows me to love others.

My heart is prepared to receive love.

I am open to the possibility of love and connection in my life.

I am confident in my ability to set healthy boundaries.

I am capable of showing up authentically in relationships.

I choose to be kind and forgiving.

I invite love and understanding into my life.

I am worthy of creating a fulfilling and joyful relationship.

I am surrounded by love, and I radiate love to everyone I encounter.

I cultivate deep, meaningful connections and trust in the divine timing of my relationships.

I forgive myself and others for any past hurt, releasing it with love, and opening myself to new and nurturing relationships.

Affirmations for Wealth

Money comes to me easily and effortlessly.

Wealth constantly flows into my life.

My life is full of abundance.

Money flows freely to me.

Money is the easiest thing for me to manifest.

I am working hard toward my ambitions.

I am capable of reaching the goals I set for my future self.

I am a magnet for success.

My work makes a difference.

I am creating the life I want.

I am in control of my financial destiny.

I am a magnet for wealth and prosperity.

I am confident and capable of achieving financial success.

I create and attract abundance in my life.

I am open to new opportunities and ideas.

I trust myself to make the right decisions for my career.

I am worthy of financial success and abundance.

I am focused on my career goals and am willing to work hard to achieve them.

I am resilient and will learn from any mistakes I make.

I am grateful for all the abundance in my life.

Affirmations for Health

I give myself permission to heal.

I appreciate and love my body.

I radiate good health.

I am calm and at peace.

I have all the energy I need to accomplish my goals.

My body is healed, restored, and filled with energy.

I am healing.

My tension is melting away.

I am doing my best, and that is enough.

I am full of energy and vitality.

My body is healthy and strong.

I am grateful for my body and mind.

I am surrounded by healing energy.

I choose to live a healthy and balanced lifestyle.

I am open to new and healthy habits.

I nourish my body with nutritious food.

I trust the wisdom of my body.

I am calm and in harmony with my body.

I am grateful for my physical and mental well-being.

Self-Care Menu

Loving actions you can do to take care of yourself.

Take a few deep breaths ....5 minutes

Stretch your body ....5 minutes

Spend some time in the sun ....5 minutes

Read a chapter of a book......................10 minutes

Meditate ....10 minutes

Burn your favorite candle......................10 minutes

Take a walk outside..............................30 minutes

Put on music and dance away...............30 minutes

Read or write poetry.............................30 minutes

Reflective Prompts for Your Journey

Welcome to the prompts section of your 369 Journal. These prompts are here to help you reflect deeply and unlock your potential using the power of 3, 6, and 9.

Take a moment to relax before you start. Approach each prompt with an open heart and mind. Write whatever comes to you, trusting your intuition.

Use these prompts to explore your thoughts, feelings, and dreams. Let them guide you to a deeper understanding of yourself and help you create the life you want.

WHY IS YOUR GOAL IMPORTANT TO YOU?

WHAT VALUES DO YOUR GOALS REPRESENT AND HOW DOES ACHIEVING
THEM CONTRIBUTE TO THE PERSON YOU ASPIRE TO BE?

IMAGINE YOUR LIFE FIVE YEARS AFTER ACHIEVING THIS GOAL. HOW HAS IT CHANGED YOUR DAILY EXPERIENCE AND YOUR RELATIONSHIPS WITH OTHERS?

DESCRIBE THE EMOTIONS YOU ASSOCIATE WITH ACHIEVING YOUR GOAL. HOW CAN YOU CULTIVATE THESE FEELINGS RIGHT NOW?

WRITE ABOUT A TIME WHEN AN UNEXPECTED SETBACK LED
TO A SURPRISING OPPORTUNITY.

WHEN FACED WITH DISAPPOINTMENT, WHAT SELF-CARE PRACTICES
HELP YOU TO RECHARGE AND REGAIN PERSPECTIVE?

REVISIT AND POSSIBLY REVISE YOUR GOALS. ARE THERE ASPECTS OF YOUR INTENTIONS THAT NEED TO BE REALIGNED WITH YOUR CURRENT SELF-UNDERSTANDING AND LIFE CIRCUMSTANCES?

WHAT PATTERNS AND SYNCHRONICITIES HAVE YOU EXPERIENCED IN YOUR LIFE?

WHAT COLOR REPRESENTS YOUR POWER?

WHAT COLOR REPRESENTS YOUR GOAL?

IF YOU HAD A MAGIC WAND, WHAT RESOURCES, OPPORTUNITIES,
AND OCCURRENCES WOULD YOU WAVE INTO YOUR LIFE?

WHAT ARE YOUR TOP FIVE STRENGTHS?

HOW CAN YOU INCORPORATE MORE JOY AND PLAYFULNESS INTO
YOUR DAILY ROUTINE?

HOW DO YOU CELEBRATE YOUR ACHIEVEMENTS, BOTH BIG AND SMALL?

WHO INSPIRES YOU AND WHY?
HOW CAN YOU EMBODY THE QUALITIES YOU ADMIRE IN THEM?

YOUR MIND IS A POWERFUL THING. WHEN YOU FILL IT WITH POSITIVE THOUGHTS, YOUR LIFE WILL START TO CHANGE.

MEDITATION FOR
OVERCOMING
CHALLENGES

SCAN HERE

"VISUALIZE YOUR
DREAM LIFE" SLEEP
MEDITATION

SCAN HERE

3
The 369 Method

What inspired actions are you taking today?

TO-DO

- [ ]
- [ ]
- [ ]
- [ ]
- [ ]
- [ ]
- [ ]
- [ ]
- [ ]
- [ ]

HOW WILL I SHOW MYSELF LOVE TODAY?

"You are the only one that creates your reality."
—RHONDA BYRNE

MORNING ☀

_____
_____
_____

AFTERNOON ☀

_____
_____
_____
_____
_____
_____

EVENING ☾

_____
_____
_____
_____
_____
_____
_____
_____

What inspired actions are you taking today?

TO-DO

- [ ]
- [ ]
- [ ]
- [ ]
- [ ]
- [ ]
- [ ]
- [ ]
- [ ]
- [ ]

HOW WILL I SHOW MYSELF LOVE TODAY?

> "Just one small positive thought in the morning
> can change your whole day."
>
> —DALAI LAMA

MORNING ☀

_____

_____

_____

AFTERNOON ☀

_____

_____

_____

_____

_____

EVENING ☾✧✧✧

_____

_____

_____

_____

_____

_____

_____

_____

What inspired actions are you taking today?

TO-DO

- [ ]
- [ ]
- [ ]
- [ ]
- [ ]
- [ ]
- [ ]
- [ ]
- [ ]
- [ ]

HOW WILL I SHOW MYSELF LOVE TODAY?

"Happy people plan actions; they don't plan results."

—DENIS WAITLEY

MORNING ☼

_____

_____

_____

AFTERNOON ☼

_____

_____

_____

_____

_____

_____

EVENING ☾ ✧✧✧

_____

_____

_____

_____

_____

_____

_____

_____

What inspired actions are you taking today?

TO-DO
- [ ]
- [ ]
- [ ]
- [ ]
- [ ]
- [ ]
- [ ]
- [ ]
- [ ]
- [ ]

HOW WILL I SHOW MYSELF LOVE TODAY?

> "The only limit to our realization of tomorrow
> will be our doubts of today."
> —FRANKLIN D. ROOSEVELT

MORNING ☀

_____

_____

_____

AFTERNOON ☀

_____

_____

_____

_____

_____

_____

EVENING ☾✧

_____

_____

_____

_____

_____

_____

_____

_____

What inspired actions are you taking today?

TO-DO

- [ ]
- [ ]
- [ ]
- [ ]
- [ ]
- [ ]
- [ ]
- [ ]
- [ ]
- [ ]

HOW WILL I SHOW MYSELF LOVE TODAY?

> "Your time is limited, so don't waste it living someone else's life."
>
> —STEVE JOBS

MORNING ☀

_____

_____

_____

AFTERNOON ☀

_____

_____

_____

_____

_____

EVENING ☾ ✧✧✧

_____

_____

_____

_____

_____

_____

_____

_____

What inspired actions are you taking today?

TO-DO

- [ ]
- [ ]
- [ ]
- [ ]
- [ ]
- [ ]
- [ ]
- [ ]
- [ ]
- [ ]

HOW WILL I SHOW MYSELF LOVE TODAY?

> "Believe you can and you're halfway there."
> —THEODORE ROOSEVELT

MORNING ☼

_____

_____

_____

AFTERNOON ☼

_____

_____

_____

_____

_____

EVENING ☾

_____

_____

_____

_____

_____

_____

_____

_____

What inspired actions are you taking today?

TO-DO

- [ ]
- [ ]
- [ ]
- [ ]
- [ ]
- [ ]
- [ ]
- [ ]
- [ ]
- [ ]

HOW WILL I SHOW MYSELF LOVE TODAY?

> "Success is not the key to happiness.
> Happiness is the key to success."
>
> —ALBERT SCHWEITZER

MORNING ☼

_____
_____
_____

AFTERNOON ☀

_____
_____
_____
_____
_____

EVENING ☾✦✧

_____
_____
_____
_____
_____
_____
_____
_____

DATE: /   /

WHAT WERE MY TOP ACHIEVEMENTS FROM LAST WEEK?

_____

_____

_____

_____

_____

HOW DID TAKING ACTION TOWARD MY GOALS FEEL?

_____

_____

_____

_____

WHAT DID NOT HAPPEN? WHAT ACTIONS CAN I TAKE TO IMPROVE?

_____

_____

_____

_____

DID I FULLY ENJOY WHAT I WAS DOING? HOW CAN I BE MORE PRESENT?

_____

_____

_____

_____

Say this affirmation:

I am dismantling all limiting beliefs in my life. I choose to feel invincible and unstoppable. I am successful in everything that I do. I show myself mercy in times of doubt or sadness. I listen to my emotions and allow myself space to feel and heal. I am aware of my patterns and take the correct actions to grow and accomplish my biggest dreams. My work is being noticed. I will concentrate. I will believe. I will take inspired action. Everything I have been manifesting exists and is appearing in my life now.

What inspired actions are you taking today?

TO-DO

- [ ]
- [ ]
- [ ]
- [ ]
- [ ]
- [ ]
- [ ]
- [ ]
- [ ]
- [ ]

HOW WILL I SHOW MYSELF LOVE TODAY?

> "Act as if what you do makes a difference. It does."
> —WILLIAM JAMES

MORNING ☀

_____
_____
_____

AFTERNOON ☀

_____
_____
_____
_____
_____

EVENING ☾✧✧

_____
_____
_____
_____
_____
_____
_____

What inspired actions are you taking today?

TO-DO

- [ ]
- [ ]
- [ ]
- [ ]
- [ ]
- [ ]
- [ ]
- [ ]
- [ ]
- [ ]

HOW WILL I SHOW MYSELF LOVE TODAY?

> "Don't watch the clock; do what it does. Keep going."
>
> —SAM LEVENSON

MORNING ☀

_____

_____

_____

AFTERNOON ☀

_____

_____

_____

_____

_____

_____

EVENING ☾✧✦✧

_____

_____

_____

_____

_____

_____

_____

_____

What inspired actions are you taking today?

TO-DO

- [ ]
- [ ]
- [ ]
- [ ]
- [ ]
- [ ]
- [ ]
- [ ]
- [ ]
- [ ]

HOW WILL I SHOW MYSELF LOVE TODAY?

> "Keep your face always toward the sunshine—and shadows will fall behind you."
>
> —WALT WHITMAN

MORNING ☀

_____
_____
_____

AFTERNOON ☀

_____
_____
_____
_____
_____

EVENING ☾✧✧✧

_____
_____
_____
_____
_____
_____
_____
_____

What inspired actions are you taking today?

TO-DO

- [ ] _____
- [ ] _____
- [ ] _____
- [ ] _____
- [ ] _____
- [ ] _____
- [ ] _____
- [ ] _____
- [ ] _____
- [ ] _____

HOW WILL I SHOW MYSELF LOVE TODAY?

_____

_____

_____

_____

_____

_____

_____

_____

> "The future belongs to those who believe in the beauty of their dreams."
>
> —ELEANOR ROOSEVELT

MORNING ☀

AFTERNOON ☀

EVENING ☾ ✦✦✦

What inspired actions are you taking today?

TO-DO

- [ ]
- [ ]
- [ ]
- [ ]
- [ ]
- [ ]
- [ ]
- [ ]
- [ ]
- [ ]

HOW WILL I SHOW MYSELF LOVE TODAY?

> "I choose to make the rest of my life the best of my life."
> —LOUISE HAY

MORNING ☼

_____
_____
_____

AFTERNOON ☀

_____
_____
_____
_____
_____

EVENING ☾✦✧✦✧

_____
_____
_____
_____
_____
_____
_____
_____

What inspired actions are you taking today?

TO-DO

- [ ]
- [ ]
- [ ]
- [ ]
- [ ]
- [ ]
- [ ]
- [ ]
- [ ]
- [ ]

HOW WILL I SHOW MYSELF LOVE TODAY?

> "Believe in yourself and all that you are. Know that there is something inside you that is greater than any obstacle."
>
> —CHRISTIAN D. LARSON

MORNING ☼

_____

_____

_____

AFTERNOON ☼

_____

_____

_____

_____

_____

EVENING ☾

_____

_____

_____

_____

_____

_____

_____

_____

What inspired actions are you taking today?

TO-DO
- [ ]
- [ ]
- [ ]
- [ ]
- [ ]
- [ ]
- [ ]
- [ ]
- [ ]
- [ ]

HOW WILL I SHOW MYSELF LOVE TODAY?

> "The best way to predict the future is to create it."
> —PETER DRUCKER

MORNING ☀

_____
_____
_____

AFTERNOON ☀

_____
_____
_____
_____
_____

EVENING ☾✧✧✧

_____
_____
_____
_____
_____
_____
_____
_____

DATE: / /

WHAT WERE MY TOP ACHIEVEMENTS FROM LAST WEEK?

_____

_____

_____

_____

_____

HOW DID TAKING ACTION TOWARD MY GOALS FEEL?

_____

_____

_____

_____

_____

WHAT DID NOT HAPPEN? WHAT ACTIONS CAN I TAKE TO IMPROVE?

_____

_____

_____

_____

_____

DID I FULLY ENJOY WHAT I WAS DOING? HOW CAN I BE MORE PRESENT?

_____

_____

_____

_____

_____

Say this affirmation:

I am attracting so much better now because I have realized that it all starts with me. Once I align with the vibrational frequency of my desired reality, it manifests itself into fruition because it already exists. All I have to do is align and be present.

What inspired actions are you taking today?

TO-DO

- [ ]
- [ ]
- [ ]
- [ ]
- [ ]
- [ ]
- [ ]
- [ ]
- [ ]
- [ ]

HOW WILL I SHOW MYSELF LOVE TODAY?

> "You are never too old to set another goal or to dream a new dream."
>
> —C. S. LEWIS

MORNING ☀

_____

_____

_____

AFTERNOON ☀

_____

_____

_____

_____

_____

EVENING ☾✦✧✧

_____

_____

_____

_____

_____

_____

_____

_____

_____

What inspired actions are you taking today?

TO-DO

- [ ] _____
- [ ] _____
- [ ] _____
- [ ] _____
- [ ] _____
- [ ] _____
- [ ] _____
- [ ] _____
- [ ] _____
- [ ] _____

HOW WILL I SHOW MYSELF LOVE TODAY?

_____
_____
_____
_____
_____
_____
_____
_____

> "What lies behind us and what lies before us are tiny matters compared to what lies within us."
>
> —RALPH WALDO EMERSON

MORNING ☼

_____

_____

_____

AFTERNOON ☼

_____

_____

_____

_____

_____

EVENING ☾ ✧ ✧

_____

_____

_____

_____

_____

_____

_____

What inspired actions are you taking today?

TO-DO

☐ _____
☐ _____
☐ _____
☐ _____
☐ _____
☐ _____
☐ _____
☐ _____
☐ _____
☐ _____

HOW WILL I SHOW MYSELF LOVE TODAY?

_____
_____
_____
_____
_____
_____
_____
_____
_____

> "The power of imagination makes us infinite."
> —JOHN MUIR

MORNING ☀

_____

_____

_____

AFTERNOON ☀

_____

_____

_____

_____

_____

EVENING ☾ ✧✦✧

_____

_____

_____

_____

_____

_____

_____

_____

_____

What inspired actions are you taking today?

TO-DO

- [ ]
- [ ]
- [ ]
- [ ]
- [ ]
- [ ]
- [ ]
- [ ]
- [ ]
- [ ]

HOW WILL I SHOW MYSELF LOVE TODAY?

> "The only way to do great work is to love what you do."
> —STEVE JOBS

MORNING ☀

_____

_____

_____

AFTERNOON ☀

_____

_____

_____

_____

_____

EVENING ☾

_____

_____

_____

_____

_____

_____

_____

_____

What inspired actions are you taking today?

TO-DO

- [ ]
- [ ]
- [ ]
- [ ]
- [ ]
- [ ]
- [ ]
- [ ]
- [ ]
- [ ]

HOW WILL I SHOW MYSELF LOVE TODAY?

> "You miss 100 percent of the shots you don't take."
> —WAYNE GRETZKY

MORNING ☼

_____

_____

_____

AFTERNOON ☼

_____

_____

_____

_____

_____

EVENING ☾ ✧ ✧

_____

_____

_____

_____

_____

_____

_____

_____

_____

What inspired actions are you taking today?

TO-DO

- [ ]
- [ ]
- [ ]
- [ ]
- [ ]
- [ ]
- [ ]
- [ ]
- [ ]
- [ ]

HOW WILL I SHOW MYSELF LOVE TODAY?

> "It does not matter how slowly you go as long as you do not stop."
>
> —CONFUCIUS

MORNING

_____

_____

_____

AFTERNOON

_____

_____

_____

_____

_____

EVENING

_____

_____

_____

_____

_____

_____

_____

What inspired actions are you taking today?

TO-DO
- [ ] _____
- [ ] _____
- [ ] _____
- [ ] _____
- [ ] _____
- [ ] _____
- [ ] _____
- [ ] _____
- [ ] _____
- [ ] _____

HOW WILL I SHOW MYSELF LOVE TODAY?

_____

_____

_____

_____

_____

_____

_____

_____

> "The mind is everything. What you think you become."
> —BUDDHA

MORNING ☀

_____

_____

_____

AFTERNOON ☀

_____

_____

_____

_____

_____

EVENING ☾ ✦

_____

_____

_____

_____

_____

_____

_____

_____

DATE: /   /

WHAT WERE MY TOP ACHIEVEMENTS FROM LAST WEEK?

_____

_____

_____

_____

_____

HOW DID TAKING ACTION TOWARD MY GOALS FEEL?

_____

_____

_____

_____

WHAT DID NOT HAPPEN? WHAT ACTIONS CAN I TAKE TO IMPROVE?

_____

_____

_____

_____

DID I FULLY ENJOY WHAT I WAS DOING? HOW CAN I BE MORE PRESENT?

_____

_____

_____

_____

_____

Say this affirmation:

I release the need to blame anyone, including myself. I am doing the best I can with the knowledge and awareness that I have. I let go of all expectations. Whatever comes up will be fulfilling. I love myself, and only good awaits me at every turn. I see the perfection in all of life and breathe love into my vision to see with clarity, compassion, and understanding.

What inspired actions are you taking today?

TO-DO
- [ ] _____
- [ ] _____
- [ ] _____
- [ ] _____
- [ ] _____
- [ ] _____
- [ ] _____
- [ ] _____
- [ ] _____
- [ ] _____

HOW WILL I SHOW MYSELF LOVE TODAY?

_____
_____
_____
_____
_____
_____
_____
_____

> "The only thing standing between you and your
> goal is the story you keep telling yourself as to
> why you can't achieve it."
>
> —JORDAN BELFORT

MORNING ☼

_____

_____

_____

AFTERNOON ☼

_____

_____

_____

_____

_____

_____

EVENING ☾ ✧✧✧

_____

_____

_____

_____

_____

_____

_____

_____

What inspired actions are you taking today?

TO-DO

- [ ] _____
- [ ] _____
- [ ] _____
- [ ] _____
- [ ] _____
- [ ] _____
- [ ] _____
- [ ] _____
- [ ] _____
- [ ] _____

HOW WILL I SHOW MYSELF LOVE TODAY?

_____
_____
_____
_____
_____
_____
_____
_____

"Don't be pushed around by the fears in your mind.
Be led by the dreams in your heart."

—ROY T. BENNETT

MORNING ☼

_____

_____

_____

AFTERNOON ☼

_____

_____

_____

_____

_____

EVENING ☾

_____

_____

_____

_____

_____

_____

_____

_____

What inspired actions are you taking today?

TO-DO
- [ ]
- [ ]
- [ ]
- [ ]
- [ ]
- [ ]
- [ ]
- [ ]
- [ ]
- [ ]

HOW WILL I SHOW MYSELF LOVE TODAY?

> "Success is walking from failure to failure with no loss of enthusiasm."
>
> —WINSTON CHURCHILL

MORNING ☀

AFTERNOON ☀

EVENING ☾✧✧

What inspired actions are you taking today?

TO-DO

- [ ] _____
- [ ] _____
- [ ] _____
- [ ] _____
- [ ] _____
- [ ] _____
- [ ] _____
- [ ] _____
- [ ] _____
- [ ] _____

HOW WILL I SHOW MYSELF LOVE TODAY?

_____

_____

_____

_____

_____

_____

_____

_____

> "Happiness is not something ready-made. It comes from your own actions."
>
> —DALAI LAMA

MORNING ☀

_____

_____

_____

AFTERNOON ☀

_____

_____

_____

_____

_____

_____

EVENING ☾

_____

_____

_____

_____

_____

_____

_____

What inspired actions are you taking today?

TO-DO

- [ ]
- [ ]
- [ ]
- [ ]
- [ ]
- [ ]
- [ ]
- [ ]
- [ ]
- [ ]

HOW WILL I SHOW MYSELF LOVE TODAY?

> "The only way to achieve the impossible is to
> believe it is possible."
>
> —LEWIS CARROLL

MORNING ☼

AFTERNOON ☼

EVENING ☾ ✧✦✧

What inspired actions are you taking today?

TO-DO

- [ ] _____
- [ ] _____
- [ ] _____
- [ ] _____
- [ ] _____
- [ ] _____
- [ ] _____
- [ ] _____
- [ ] _____
- [ ] _____

HOW WILL I SHOW MYSELF LOVE TODAY?

_____
_____
_____
_____
_____
_____
_____
_____

"Dream big and dare to fail."
—NORMAN VAUGHAN

MORNING ☀

_____

_____

_____

AFTERNOON ☀

_____

_____

_____

_____

_____

_____

EVENING ☾ ✧

_____

_____

_____

_____

_____

_____

_____

_____

_____

What inspired actions are you taking today?

TO-DO

- [ ] _____
- [ ] _____
- [ ] _____
- [ ] _____
- [ ] _____
- [ ] _____
- [ ] _____
- [ ] _____
- [ ] _____
- [ ] _____

HOW WILL I SHOW MYSELF LOVE TODAY?

_____
_____
_____
_____
_____
_____
_____
_____

> "Don't wait. The time will never be just right."
>
> —NAPOLEON HILL

MORNING ☼
_____
_____
_____

AFTERNOON ☼
_____
_____
_____
_____
_____

EVENING ☾✦✧
_____
_____
_____
_____
_____
_____
_____

DATE: /   /

WHAT WERE MY TOP ACHIEVEMENTS FROM LAST WEEK?

_____

_____

_____

_____

_____

HOW DID TAKING ACTION TOWARD MY GOALS FEEL?

_____

_____

_____

_____

_____

WHAT DID NOT HAPPEN? WHAT ACTIONS CAN I TAKE TO IMPROVE?

_____

_____

_____

_____

_____

DID I FULLY ENJOY WHAT I WAS DOING? HOW CAN I BE MORE PRESENT?

_____

_____

_____

_____

_____

Look within yourself.

Look at all you've endured.

Look at all the love you hold.

Realize your power.

Realize your strength.

Realize your unlimited capability.

Remember yourself.

What inspired actions are you taking today?

TO-DO

- [ ]
- [ ]
- [ ]
- [ ]
- [ ]
- [ ]
- [ ]
- [ ]
- [ ]
- [ ]

HOW WILL I SHOW MYSELF LOVE TODAY?

> "Everything you've ever wanted is on the other side of fear."
> —GEORGE ADAIR

MORNING ☀

_____
_____
_____

AFTERNOON ☀

_____
_____
_____
_____
_____

EVENING ☾✧✧

_____
_____
_____
_____
_____
_____
_____
_____

What inspired actions are you taking today?

TO-DO

- [ ]
- [ ]
- [ ]
- [ ]
- [ ]
- [ ]
- [ ]
- [ ]
- [ ]
- [ ]

HOW WILL I SHOW MYSELF LOVE TODAY?

"Keep your eyes on the stars and your feet on the ground."
—THEODORE ROOSEVELT

MORNING ☀

_____
_____
_____

AFTERNOON ☀

_____
_____
_____
_____
_____

EVENING ☽ ✧

_____
_____
_____
_____
_____
_____
_____
_____
_____

What inspired actions are you taking today?

TO-DO

- [ ]
- [ ]
- [ ]
- [ ]
- [ ]
- [ ]
- [ ]
- [ ]
- [ ]
- [ ]

HOW WILL I SHOW MYSELF LOVE TODAY?

> "We may encounter many defeats, but we must not be defeated."
> —MAYA ANGELOU

MORNING ☀

_____

_____

_____

AFTERNOON ☀

_____

_____

_____

_____

_____

_____

EVENING ☾✧✧

_____

_____

_____

_____

_____

_____

_____

_____

What inspired actions are you taking today?

TO-DO

- [ ]
- [ ]
- [ ]
- [ ]
- [ ]
- [ ]
- [ ]
- [ ]
- [ ]
- [ ]

HOW WILL I SHOW MYSELF LOVE TODAY?

> "The more you praise and celebrate your life, the more there is in life to celebrate."
>
> —OPRAH WINFREY

MORNING ☀

_____

_____

_____

AFTERNOON ☀

_____

_____

_____

_____

_____

EVENING ☾✧✩✧

_____

_____

_____

_____

_____

_____

_____

_____

_____

What inspired actions are you taking today?

TO-DO

- [ ]
- [ ]
- [ ]
- [ ]
- [ ]
- [ ]
- [ ]
- [ ]
- [ ]
- [ ]

HOW WILL I SHOW MYSELF LOVE TODAY?

> "The only person you are destined to become is the person you decide to be."
>
> —RALPH WALDO EMERSON

MORNING ☀

_____
_____
_____

AFTERNOON ☀

_____
_____
_____
_____
_____

EVENING ☾✦✧

_____
_____
_____
_____
_____
_____
_____

What inspired actions are you taking today?

TO-DO

- [ ] _____
- [ ] _____
- [ ] _____
- [ ] _____
- [ ] _____
- [ ] _____
- [ ] _____
- [ ] _____
- [ ] _____
- [ ] _____

HOW WILL I SHOW MYSELF LOVE TODAY?

_____
_____
_____
_____
_____
_____
_____
_____
_____

> "Happiness is not by chance, but by choice."
> —JIM ROHN

MORNING ☀

_____

_____

_____

AFTERNOON ☀

_____

_____

_____

_____

_____

EVENING ☽

_____

_____

_____

_____

_____

_____

_____

What inspired actions are you taking today?

TO-DO

- [ ]
- [ ]
- [ ]
- [ ]
- [ ]
- [ ]
- [ ]
- [ ]
- [ ]
- [ ]

HOW WILL I SHOW MYSELF LOVE TODAY?

> "Life is 10 percent what happens to us and
> 90 percent how we react to it."
>
> —CHARLES R. SWINDOLL

MORNING ☀

_____

_____

_____

AFTERNOON ☀

_____

_____

_____

_____

_____

EVENING ☾✧✧

_____

_____

_____

_____

_____

_____

_____

_____

DATE: /   /

WHAT WERE MY TOP ACHIEVEMENTS FROM LAST WEEK?

_____

_____

_____

_____

_____

HOW DID TAKING ACTION TOWARD MY GOALS FEEL?

_____

_____

_____

_____

_____

WHAT DID NOT HAPPEN? WHAT ACTIONS CAN I TAKE TO IMPROVE?

_____

_____

_____

_____

_____

DID I FULLY ENJOY WHAT I WAS DOING? HOW CAN I BE MORE PRESENT?

_____

_____

_____

_____

_____

Avalanches of things you've been wanting are going to end up in your experience. And it will happen when you stop worrying about its *not* happening.

Find the positive "what if" game instead of the negative "what if" game.

—ABRAHAM-HICKS

What inspired actions are you taking today?

TO-DO

- [ ] _____
- [ ] _____
- [ ] _____
- [ ] _____
- [ ] _____
- [ ] _____
- [ ] _____
- [ ] _____
- [ ] _____
- [ ] _____

HOW WILL I SHOW MYSELF LOVE TODAY?

_____

_____

_____

_____

_____

_____

_____

_____

> "Start where you are. Use what you have. Do what you can."
> —ARTHUR ASHE

MORNING ☼

_____
_____
_____

AFTERNOON ☼

_____
_____
_____
_____
_____
_____

EVENING ☾✧✦✧

_____
_____
_____
_____
_____
_____
_____
_____
_____

What inspired actions are you taking today?

TO-DO

- [ ]
- [ ]
- [ ]
- [ ]
- [ ]
- [ ]
- [ ]
- [ ]
- [ ]
- [ ]

HOW WILL I SHOW MYSELF LOVE TODAY?

> "The only place where success comes before work is in the dictionary."
>
> —VIDAL SASSOON

MORNING ☀

_____

_____

_____

AFTERNOON ☀

_____

_____

_____

_____

_____

EVENING ☾

_____

_____

_____

_____

_____

_____

_____

_____

What inspired actions are you taking today?

TO-DO
- [ ] _____
- [ ] _____
- [ ] _____
- [ ] _____
- [ ] _____
- [ ] _____
- [ ] _____
- [ ] _____
- [ ] _____
- [ ] _____

HOW WILL I SHOW MYSELF LOVE TODAY?

_____

_____

_____

_____

_____

_____

_____

_____

"Success is not how high you have climbed,
but how you make a positive difference to the world."

—ROY T. BENNETT

MORNING ☀

_____

_____

_____

AFTERNOON ☀

_____

_____

_____

_____

EVENING ☾

_____

_____

_____

_____

_____

_____

_____

What inspired actions are you taking today?

TO-DO
- [ ]
- [ ]
- [ ]
- [ ]
- [ ]
- [ ]
- [ ]
- [ ]
- [ ]
- [ ]

HOW WILL I SHOW MYSELF LOVE TODAY?

"The best time to plant a tree was twenty years ago.
The second-best time is now."

—CHINESE PROVERB

MORNING ☼

_____

_____

_____

AFTERNOON ☼

_____

_____

_____

_____

_____

EVENING ☾ ✧✧✧

_____

_____

_____

_____

_____

_____

_____

_____

What inspired actions are you taking today?

TO-DO
- [ ]
- [ ]
- [ ]
- [ ]
- [ ]
- [ ]
- [ ]
- [ ]
- [ ]
- [ ]

HOW WILL I SHOW MYSELF LOVE TODAY?

> "The way to get started is to quit talking and begin doing."
> —WALT DISNEY

MORNING ☀

_____
_____
_____

AFTERNOON ☀

_____
_____
_____
_____
_____

EVENING ☾ ✦

_____
_____
_____
_____
_____
_____
_____
_____

What inspired actions are you taking today?

TO-DO
- [ ]
- [ ]
- [ ]
- [ ]
- [ ]
- [ ]
- [ ]
- [ ]
- [ ]
- [ ]

HOW WILL I SHOW MYSELF LOVE TODAY?

> "You may have to fight a battle more than once to win it."
> —MARGARET THATCHER

MORNING ☀

_____

_____

_____

AFTERNOON ☀

_____

_____

_____

_____

_____

EVENING ☾✦✧✦

_____

_____

_____

_____

_____

_____

_____

_____

What inspired actions are you taking today?

TO-DO

- [ ]
- [ ]
- [ ]
- [ ]
- [ ]
- [ ]
- [ ]
- [ ]
- [ ]
- [ ]

HOW WILL I SHOW MYSELF LOVE TODAY?

> "You become what you believe."
> —OPRAH WINFREY

MORNING ☀

_____

_____

_____

AFTERNOON ☀

_____

_____

_____

_____

_____

EVENING ☾ ✦ ✦

_____

_____

_____

_____

_____

_____

_____

_____

DATE: / /

WHAT WERE MY TOP ACHIEVEMENTS FROM LAST WEEK?

_____

_____

_____

_____

_____

HOW DID TAKING ACTION TOWARD MY GOALS FEEL?

_____

_____

_____

_____

WHAT DID NOT HAPPEN? WHAT ACTIONS CAN I TAKE TO IMPROVE?

_____

_____

_____

_____

DID I FULLY ENJOY WHAT I WAS DOING? HOW CAN I BE MORE PRESENT?

_____

_____

_____

_____

_____

Say this affirmation:

I radiate love, and love fills my life.

I am accomplishing my greatest dreams easily and seamlessly. I am in the process of positive changes, and I can feel my emotions shifting for the better. Money is energy, and it is on its way to me. Money constantly flows into my life because my relationship with it is positive and magnetic.

I am confident in my ability to persevere and stay consistent. I am my highest self.

What inspired actions are you taking today?

TO-DO

- [ ] _____
- [ ] _____
- [ ] _____
- [ ] _____
- [ ] _____
- [ ] _____
- [ ] _____
- [ ] _____
- [ ] _____
- [ ] _____

HOW WILL I SHOW MYSELF LOVE TODAY?

_____
_____
_____
_____
_____
_____
_____
_____

> "The best way to predict the future is to invent it."
> —ALAN KAY

MORNING ☀

_____

_____

_____

AFTERNOON ☼

_____

_____

_____

_____

_____

EVENING ☾✦✧✧

_____

_____

_____

_____

_____

_____

_____

_____

What inspired actions are you taking today?

TO-DO
- [ ]
- [ ]
- [ ]
- [ ]
- [ ]
- [ ]
- [ ]
- [ ]
- [ ]
- [ ]

HOW WILL I SHOW MYSELF LOVE TODAY?

> "Do what you can, with what you have, where you are."
> —THEODORE ROOSEVELT

MORNING ☼

AFTERNOON ☼

EVENING ☾ ✧✧

What inspired actions are you taking today?

TO-DO

- [ ] _____
- [ ] _____
- [ ] _____
- [ ] _____
- [ ] _____
- [ ] _____
- [ ] _____
- [ ] _____
- [ ] _____
- [ ] _____

HOW WILL I SHOW MYSELF LOVE TODAY?

_____
_____
_____
_____
_____
_____
_____
_____

> "Don't let yesterday take up too much of today."
>
> —WILL ROGERS

MORNING ☀

_____
_____
_____

AFTERNOON ☀

_____
_____
_____
_____
_____

EVENING ☾✦✧

_____
_____
_____
_____
_____
_____
_____
_____

What inspired actions are you taking today?

TO-DO

- [ ]
- [ ]
- [ ]
- [ ]
- [ ]
- [ ]
- [ ]
- [ ]
- [ ]
- [ ]

HOW WILL I SHOW MYSELF LOVE TODAY?

> "I have not failed. I've just found ten thousand ways that won't work."
>
> —THOMAS EDISON

MORNING ☼

_____

_____

_____

AFTERNOON ☀

_____

_____

_____

_____

_____

EVENING ☾✧✦

_____

_____

_____

_____

_____

_____

_____

_____

What inspired actions are you taking today?

TO-DO

- [ ]
- [ ]
- [ ]
- [ ]
- [ ]
- [ ]
- [ ]
- [ ]
- [ ]
- [ ]

HOW WILL I SHOW MYSELF LOVE TODAY?

"It's not whether you get knocked down; it's whether you get up."
—VINCE LOMBARDI

MORNING ☀

_____

_____

_____

AFTERNOON ☀

_____

_____

_____

_____

_____

EVENING ☾

_____

_____

_____

_____

_____

_____

What inspired actions are you taking today?

TO-DO

- [ ]
- [ ]
- [ ]
- [ ]
- [ ]
- [ ]
- [ ]
- [ ]
- [ ]
- [ ]

HOW WILL I SHOW MYSELF LOVE TODAY?

> "Failure will never overtake me if my
> determination to succeed is strong enough."
>
> —OG MANDINO

MORNING

_____
_____
_____

AFTERNOON

_____
_____
_____
_____
_____
_____

EVENING

_____
_____
_____
_____
_____
_____
_____
_____

What inspired actions are you taking today?

TO-DO

- [ ] _____
- [ ] _____
- [ ] _____
- [ ] _____
- [ ] _____
- [ ] _____
- [ ] _____
- [ ] _____
- [ ] _____
- [ ] _____

HOW WILL I SHOW MYSELF LOVE TODAY?

_____

_____

_____

_____

_____

_____

_____

_____

_____

> "Knowing is not enough; we must apply.
> Wishing is not enough; we must do."
>
> —JOHANN WOLFGANG VON GOETHE

MORNING ☀

_____

_____

_____

AFTERNOON ☀

_____

_____

_____

_____

_____

EVENING ☾✦✧✦

_____

_____

_____

_____

_____

_____

_____

_____

DATE: /   /

WHAT WERE MY TOP ACHIEVEMENTS FROM LAST WEEK?

_____

_____

_____

_____

_____

HOW DID TAKING ACTION TOWARD MY GOALS FEEL?

_____

_____

_____

_____

_____

WHAT DID NOT HAPPEN? WHAT ACTIONS CAN I TAKE TO IMPROVE?

_____

_____

_____

_____

_____

DID I FULLY ENJOY WHAT I WAS DOING? HOW CAN I BE MORE PRESENT?

_____

_____

_____

_____

_____

Say this affirmation:

I am the most powerful I have ever been. I am walking into the wealthiest and healthiest version of myself.

Everything I desire is on its way to me because everything I desire is already mine.

What inspired actions are you taking today?

TO-DO

- [ ]
- [ ]
- [ ]
- [ ]
- [ ]
- [ ]
- [ ]
- [ ]
- [ ]
- [ ]

HOW WILL I SHOW MYSELF LOVE TODAY?

> "Every thought we think is creating our future."
> —LOUISE HAY

MORNING ☀

_____

_____

_____

AFTERNOON ☀

_____

_____

_____

_____

_____

EVENING ☾ ✧

_____

_____

_____

_____

_____

_____

_____

_____

What inspired actions are you taking today?

TO-DO
- [ ] _____
- [ ] _____
- [ ] _____
- [ ] _____
- [ ] _____
- [ ] _____
- [ ] _____
- [ ] _____
- [ ] _____
- [ ] _____

HOW WILL I SHOW MYSELF LOVE TODAY?

_____
_____
_____
_____
_____
_____
_____
_____

"Gratitude is the greatest multiplier."

—RHONDA BYRNE

MORNING ☀️

_____

_____

_____

AFTERNOON ☀️

_____

_____

_____

_____

_____

EVENING 🌙✨

_____

_____

_____

_____

_____

_____

_____

_____

What inspired actions are you taking today?

TO-DO

- [ ] _____
- [ ] _____
- [ ] _____
- [ ] _____
- [ ] _____
- [ ] _____
- [ ] _____
- [ ] _____
- [ ] _____
- [ ] _____

HOW WILL I SHOW MYSELF LOVE TODAY?

_____

_____

_____

_____

_____

_____

_____

_____

> "You are the designer of your destiny;
> you are the author of your story."
>
> —LISA NICHOLS

MORNING ☀

_____
_____
_____

AFTERNOON ☀

_____
_____
_____
_____
_____

EVENING ☾ ✧✧✧

_____
_____
_____
_____
_____
_____
_____
_____

What inspired actions are you taking today?

TO-DO

☐ _____
☐ _____
☐ _____
☐ _____
☐ _____
☐ _____
☐ _____
☐ _____
☐ _____
☐ _____

HOW WILL I SHOW MYSELF LOVE TODAY?

_____
_____
_____
_____
_____
_____
_____
_____

"What you think, you create. What you feel, you attract. What you imagine, you become."

—RHONDA BYRNE

MORNING ☼

_____

_____

_____

AFTERNOON ☼

_____

_____

_____

_____

_____

EVENING ☾✧✧

_____

_____

_____

_____

_____

_____

_____

What inspired actions are you taking today?

TO-DO

- [ ] _____
- [ ] _____
- [ ] _____
- [ ] _____
- [ ] _____
- [ ] _____
- [ ] _____
- [ ] _____
- [ ] _____
- [ ] _____

HOW WILL I SHOW MYSELF LOVE TODAY?

_____
_____
_____
_____
_____
_____
_____
_____
_____

"With the new day comes new strength and new thoughts."
—ELEANOR ROOSEVELT

MORNING ☀

_____

_____

_____

AFTERNOON ☀

_____

_____

_____

_____

_____

EVENING ☾

_____

_____

_____

_____

_____

_____

_____

What inspired actions are you taking today?

TO-DO

- [ ] _____
- [ ] _____
- [ ] _____
- [ ] _____
- [ ] _____
- [ ] _____
- [ ] _____
- [ ] _____
- [ ] _____
- [ ] _____

HOW WILL I SHOW MYSELF LOVE TODAY?

_____

_____

_____

_____

_____

_____

_____

_____

"We generate fears while we sit. We overcome them by action."

—DR. HENRY LINK

MORNING ☀

_____

_____

_____

AFTERNOON ☀

_____

_____

_____

_____

_____

EVENING ☾ ✧

_____

_____

_____

_____

_____

_____

_____

What inspired actions are you taking today?

TO-DO

- [ ]
- [ ]
- [ ]
- [ ]
- [ ]
- [ ]
- [ ]
- [ ]
- [ ]
- [ ]

HOW WILL I SHOW MYSELF LOVE TODAY?

"Whether you think you can or think you can't, you're right."

—HENRY FORD

MORNING ☼

_____

_____

_____

AFTERNOON ☼

_____

_____

_____

_____

_____

EVENING ☾ ✧✩✧

_____

_____

_____

_____

_____

_____

_____

_____

DATE: /   /

WHAT WERE MY TOP ACHIEVEMENTS FROM LAST WEEK?

_____

_____

_____

_____

_____

HOW DID TAKING ACTION TOWARD MY GOALS FEEL?

_____

_____

_____

_____

_____

WHAT DID NOT HAPPEN? WHAT ACTIONS CAN I TAKE TO IMPROVE?

_____

_____

_____

_____

_____

DID I FULLY ENJOY WHAT I WAS DOING? HOW CAN I BE MORE PRESENT?

_____

_____

_____

_____

_____

Say this affirmation:

The thoughts I think and the words I speak consciously shift my experiences. I trust my inner wisdom. My intuition is always on my side, and I trust it to always be there. I am safe and willing to forgive others. I am not limited by any past thinking, and I choose my thoughts with care. I have new insights and new ways of looking at the world, which allow me to change and grow. I am so grateful for the physical reality around me, and for the love and hope I hold inside of me. I choose balance, harmony, and peace, and I express it in my life.

What inspired actions are you taking today?

TO-DO

- [ ]
- [ ]
- [ ]
- [ ]
- [ ]
- [ ]
- [ ]
- [ ]
- [ ]
- [ ]

HOW WILL I SHOW MYSELF LOVE TODAY?

> "What you get by achieving your goals is not as important as what you become by achieving your goals."
> —ZIG ZIGLAR

MORNING ☀

_____

_____

_____

AFTERNOON ☀

_____

_____

_____

_____

_____

EVENING ☾

_____

_____

_____

_____

_____

_____

_____

_____

What inspired actions are you taking today?

TO-DO

- [ ]
- [ ]
- [ ]
- [ ]
- [ ]
- [ ]
- [ ]
- [ ]
- [ ]
- [ ]

HOW WILL I SHOW MYSELF LOVE TODAY?

"If you really look closely, most overnight successes took a long time."

—STEVE JOBS

MORNING ☼

_____

_____

_____

AFTERNOON ☼

_____

_____

_____

_____

_____

EVENING ☾✧✧✧

_____

_____

_____

_____

_____

_____

_____

_____

What inspired actions are you taking today?

TO-DO

- [ ]
- [ ]
- [ ]
- [ ]
- [ ]
- [ ]
- [ ]
- [ ]
- [ ]
- [ ]

HOW WILL I SHOW MYSELF LOVE TODAY?

> "Don't let the fear of losing be greater than the excitement of winning."
>
> —ROBERT KIYOSAKI

MORNING ☀

_____

_____

_____

AFTERNOON ☀

_____

_____

_____

_____

_____

EVENING ☾✦✧

_____

_____

_____

_____

_____

_____

_____

What inspired actions are you taking today?

TO-DO

☐ _____

☐ _____

☐ _____

☐ _____

☐ _____

☐ _____

☐ _____

☐ _____

☐ _____

☐ _____

HOW WILL I SHOW MYSELF LOVE TODAY?

_____

_____

_____

_____

_____

_____

_____

_____

_____

"You don't have to be great to start, but you have to start to be great."

—ZIG ZIGLAR

MORNING ☼

_____
_____
_____
_____

AFTERNOON ☼

_____
_____
_____
_____
_____
_____

EVENING ☾✧✧

_____
_____
_____
_____
_____
_____
_____
_____
_____

What inspired actions are you taking today?

TO-DO

- [ ]
- [ ]
- [ ]
- [ ]
- [ ]
- [ ]
- [ ]
- [ ]
- [ ]
- [ ]

HOW WILL I SHOW MYSELF LOVE TODAY?

> "A journey of a thousand miles begins with a single step."
>
> —LAO TZU

MORNING ☼

AFTERNOON ☼

EVENING ☾ ✧✧✧

What inspired actions are you taking today?

TO-DO

- [ ]
- [ ]
- [ ]
- [ ]
- [ ]
- [ ]
- [ ]
- [ ]
- [ ]
- [ ]

HOW WILL I SHOW MYSELF LOVE TODAY?

"Don't let what you cannot do interfere with what you can do."
—JOHN R. WOODEN

MORNING ☼

_____

_____

_____

AFTERNOON ☼

_____

_____

_____

_____

_____

_____

EVENING ☾

_____

_____

_____

_____

_____

_____

_____

_____

What inspired actions are you taking today?

TO-DO
- [ ] _____
- [ ] _____
- [ ] _____
- [ ] _____
- [ ] _____
- [ ] _____
- [ ] _____
- [ ] _____
- [ ] _____
- [ ] _____

HOW WILL I SHOW MYSELF LOVE TODAY?

_____
_____
_____
_____
_____
_____
_____
_____

> "Don't wait for opportunity. Create it."
> —GEORGE BERNARD SHAW

MORNING ☀

_____

_____

_____

AFTERNOON ☀

_____

_____

_____

_____

_____

EVENING ☾✧✧✧

_____

_____

_____

_____

_____

_____

_____

DATE: /   /

WHAT WERE MY TOP ACHIEVEMENTS FROM LAST WEEK?

_____

_____

_____

_____

_____

HOW DID TAKING ACTION TOWARD MY GOALS FEEL?

_____

_____

_____

_____

_____

WHAT DID NOT HAPPEN? WHAT ACTIONS CAN I TAKE TO IMPROVE?

_____

_____

_____

_____

_____

DID I FULLY ENJOY WHAT I WAS DOING? HOW CAN I BE MORE PRESENT?

_____

_____

_____

_____

_____

Say this affirmation:

I am called to make positive changes in my life.

I am deserving of love, happiness, and health.

I am gentle with myself during this transition period. I have a clear vision of the direction my life is going in, and my heart is centered.

I take it one day at a time.

What inspired actions are you taking today?

TO-DO

- [ ]
- [ ]
- [ ]
- [ ]
- [ ]
- [ ]
- [ ]
- [ ]
- [ ]
- [ ]

HOW WILL I SHOW MYSELF LOVE TODAY?

> "The best way out is always through."
> —ROBERT FROST

MORNING ☀

_____

_____

_____

AFTERNOON ☀

_____

_____

_____

_____

_____

EVENING ☾✧✦

_____

_____

_____

_____

_____

_____

_____

_____

_____

What inspired actions are you taking today?

TO-DO

- [ ] _____
- [ ] _____
- [ ] _____
- [ ] _____
- [ ] _____
- [ ] _____
- [ ] _____
- [ ] _____
- [ ] _____
- [ ] _____

HOW WILL I SHOW MYSELF LOVE TODAY?

_____
_____
_____
_____
_____
_____
_____
_____
_____

> "Don't count the days, make the days count."
> —MUHAMMAD ALI

MORNING ☀

_____
_____
_____

AFTERNOON ☀

_____
_____
_____
_____
_____

EVENING ☾

_____
_____
_____
_____
_____
_____
_____
_____

What inspired actions are you taking today?

TO-DO

- [ ] _____
- [ ] _____
- [ ] _____
- [ ] _____
- [ ] _____
- [ ] _____
- [ ] _____
- [ ] _____
- [ ] _____
- [ ] _____

HOW WILL I SHOW MYSELF LOVE TODAY?

_____
_____
_____
_____
_____
_____
_____
_____
_____

> "It always seems impossible until it's done."
> —NELSON MANDELA

MORNING ☀

AFTERNOON ☀

EVENING ☾ ✧✧✧

What inspired actions are you taking today?

TO-DO

- [ ] _____
- [ ] _____
- [ ] _____
- [ ] _____
- [ ] _____
- [ ] _____
- [ ] _____
- [ ] _____
- [ ] _____
- [ ] _____

HOW WILL I SHOW MYSELF LOVE TODAY?

_____

_____

_____

_____

_____

_____

_____

_____

> "You must be the change you wish to see in the world."
> —MAHATMA GANDHI

MORNING ☀

_____

_____

_____

AFTERNOON ☀

_____

_____

_____

_____

EVENING ☾✦✧✦

_____

_____

_____

_____

_____

_____

_____

_____

What inspired actions are you taking today?

TO-DO

- [ ] _____
- [ ] _____
- [ ] _____
- [ ] _____
- [ ] _____
- [ ] _____
- [ ] _____
- [ ] _____
- [ ] _____
- [ ] _____

HOW WILL I SHOW MYSELF LOVE TODAY?

_____
_____
_____
_____
_____
_____
_____
_____
_____

> "I am in the right place, at the right time, doing the right thing."
> —LOUISE HAY

MORNING ☼

_____

_____

_____

AFTERNOON ☼

_____

_____

_____

_____

_____

EVENING ☾ ✧✧✧

_____

_____

_____

_____

_____

_____

_____

_____

What inspired actions are you taking today?

TO-DO

- [ ]
- [ ]
- [ ]
- [ ]
- [ ]
- [ ]
- [ ]
- [ ]
- [ ]
- [ ]

HOW WILL I SHOW MYSELF LOVE TODAY?

> "Imagination is everything. It is the preview of
> life's coming attractions."
>
> —ALBERT EINSTEIN

MORNING ☀

_____
_____
_____

AFTERNOON ☀

_____
_____
_____
_____
_____

EVENING ☾ ✧

_____
_____
_____
_____
_____
_____
_____

What inspired actions are you taking today?

TO-DO

- [ ]
- [ ]
- [ ]
- [ ]
- [ ]
- [ ]
- [ ]
- [ ]
- [ ]
- [ ]

HOW WILL I SHOW MYSELF LOVE TODAY?

> "Whatever the mind of man can conceive and believe,
> it can achieve."
>
> —NAPOLEON HILL

MORNING ☼

AFTERNOON ☼

EVENING ☾ ✧✧✧

DATE: /   /

WHAT WERE MY TOP ACHIEVEMENTS FROM LAST WEEK?

_____

_____

_____

_____

_____

HOW DID TAKING ACTION TOWARD MY GOALS FEEL?

_____

_____

_____

_____

_____

WHAT DID NOT HAPPEN? WHAT ACTIONS CAN I TAKE TO IMPROVE?

_____

_____

_____

_____

_____

DID I FULLY ENJOY WHAT I WAS DOING? HOW CAN I BE MORE PRESENT?

_____

_____

_____

_____

_____

Say this affirmation:

Today, I will celebrate everything I have accomplished. I will rejoice in all the goodness this world has within it. I will consciously remember all the peace and happiness I've experienced in this life, and I will use those emotions as a compass to be my greatest, most abundant self.

DOWNLOAD
the APP

SCAN HERE

WHERE TECHNOLOGY
MEETS INNER TRANSFORMATION.

- Track triggers

- Check in feelings

- Journal prompts

- Healing exercises

- View emotional patterns over time